ONE MAN'S OPINION

A Suggested Rewrite for the Constitution of the United States

by

William D. Kuehler, Jr.

DORRANCE PUBLISHING CO., INC.
PITTSBURGH, PENNSYLVANIA 15222

ISBN: 978-1-4349-0946-6
eISBN: 978-1-4349-5788-7
Printed in the United States of America

First Printing

For more information or to order additional books, please contact:
Dorrance Publishing Co., Inc.
701 Smithfield Street
Pittsburgh, Pennsylvania 15222
U.S.A.
1-800-788-7654
www.dorrancebookstore.com

This book is dedicated to the 2,000 years of humanity, who made the ultimate sacrifice for freedom and who would not like to see their sacrifices made hollow by the gradual decay of the American dream. The influence of American democracy upon the world scene is well known. The impact of our laws and free market allowed America to enjoy a degree of wealth and luxury for all, instead of just a privileged few; however, the one fault of America's democracy is the pandering by Congress, to the general public, for ever-increasing spending on social programs. The unbalanced budgets will eat away at America's future till its existence is threatened. The dreams of the past generation, for liberty and rights for all, should not be replaced by the yoke of financial incompetence on the part of a misguided Congress. I attempt to correct the situation by writing a new constitution and in so doing correct many of the inadequacies in the 1787 version. A piece of legislation or an amendment to the existing constitution will be insufficient. Indeed, with a new constitution, the American dream will carry on and the efforts and sacrifices of our ancestors will not be in vain.

PREFACE

The genius of man that enabled him to formulate the American Constitution of 1787 gave rise to the world's first great democracy. For over two hundred years, it functioned in a manner that provided for its people and fended off external threats. In that respect, the Constitution has become a monument to the mind of man, in that it has outlasted those governments in existence when it was first written and those who sought to conquer it. Yet, the Constitution, which has been amended many times, has proven perishable under the unstoppable march of time. It has become apparent that much was not included in the 1787 Constitution, probably by the inadequacies of the authors or by compromises of the Constitutional Convention. Some of these inadequacies, like the failure to stipulate a balanced Federal budget, may have been because, at that time, it would be unthinkable not to have a balanced budget. However, this document, written on parchment—the skin of an animal—had a value far beyond its material value but was valued for the words written upon it. Where the barbarians, who conquered Rome, were concerned with the spoils and luxuries they could acquire, the enemies of the United States ultimately were concerned with the destruction of the meaning of these words, for these words were what they feared the most: liberty and the right of self-determination—the right to choose ones leadership and have a representative form of government based upon written law. The idea of a democratic government sounded the death knoll of the dictator, the monarch, and the theocracy.

The perishability of our Constitution, and ultimately of our way of life, appears to be of our own making, due to our failure to properly manage the financial affairs of the nation. We have entered our dark period where the survival of our democracy rests on the edge. The cause of our destruction may well be recorded by historians as our own domestic incompetence. All is not lost yet, however, and there is still hope. By correcting the inadequacies in the Constitution and forcing governmental behavior to a more logical diligence, we can look forward to another two hundred years of prosperity. Therefore, the standards put forth in this document are both necessary and reasonable for sustaining the American democracy. It is because of these constitutional inadequacies that I put forward my opinions as to a rewrite of the United States Constitution. This constitution is the opinion of a common man.

PREAMBLE

We the people of the United States, in recognition of the service of the Constitution of 1787, hereby ordain and establish a new constitution founded upon the just principles and values of the original, but modified to include those doctrines that through the centuries have proven missing and needed, and therefore command inclusion within a new constitution. In humble recognition to those who have made the ultimate sacrifice in defending the American way of life, we establish this new constitution for the United States.

*As I compose this new constitution, I will use the framework of the existing Constitution in order to build a new one. This is designed to provide some level of comfort to those reviewing this new constitution that I have expanded upon, adding to a framework that has worked for two hundred years. Passages from the original Constitution will be written in regular Font with modifications or additions in **Bold** Font. My comments will be in italics. Many parts from the Bill of Rights will be inserted into this new constitution, as appropriate, and some new amendments are proposed.*

THE CONSTITUTION OF THE UNITED STATES OF AMERICA

Article 1
Section 1: All legislative powers herein granted shall be vested in a Congress of the United States, consisting of a House of Representatives.

The existence of a Senate is abolished in this constitution. It is felt that the reason for the Senate was that the uneducated rabble, in the House of Representatives, could not be trusted and that the landed gentry needed to maintain a finger on the pulse of the government. The original framers of the Constitution tended therefore to agree with the English rational for the existence of a House of Lords. In today's terms, the existence of the two houses adds unnecessary delay, disruption, and complexity in the affairs of the government. By eliminating the Senate, the activities of the legislature are thus streamlined.

Section 2: The House of Representatives shall be chosen every fourth year by popular vote of the people of the states. No person shall be a representative who shall not have attained the age of twenty-five years and been ten years a citizen of the United States and who when elected shall have been a resident of the state from which they are running for a period of five years.

It is felt that the present two-year term is too short. I have increased the citizenship requirement from seven years to ten and have added a residency requirement for the state from which the representative is running for election. The residency requirement is to eliminate carpetbagger politicians of notoriety from running in another state, as we have seen in recent history.

Section 3: The number of representatives that makes up the House of Representatives shall be four hundred and ninety-nine, and their number shall be apportioned among the states based on the last census. No state shall have less than two representatives.

The United States government shall take a census of the population every ten years. The nation's population divided by four hundred and ninety-nine shall determine the population density per representative. Each state's population shall be divided by this density number to determine the number of representatives to be elected from each state. If the number is fractionally larger than one-half, then the number is to be rounded up to the next whole number, and if it is lower than one-half, it is to be dropped. Congressional districts are to be determined using the presently existing county borders. No arbitrary district geometry is to be used. If the number of representatives does not match the number of counties and their population, then counties will be shared by representatives.

The specific purpose of this procedure is to eliminate gerrymandering by one political party for its own advantage.

In order to ensure fair and impartial representation and eliminate the process known as gerrymandering in the determination of state districts for state legislatures, the representative bodies of the respective states are to have their state districts determined by county borders as well. No physically disconnected counties are to be combined into a district. County borders are not to be changed as a method to circumvent this attempt to eliminate gerrymandering. County borders shall not be changed during the transition period for full implementation of this constitution. If the respective states have manipulated county borders during the transition period, they are to be reset to their former borders at the end of the transition period. If the number of state representatives does not match the number of counties and their population, then counties will be shared with other state representatives.

When vacancies happen in the representation from any state, the governor of that state shall appoint a temporary replacement. The replacement shall be from the same political party. Spouses or members of the immediate family of the representative who is no longer able to serve are not allowed to be appointed as a replacement.

The House of Representatives shall choose a Speaker and other officers as needed to fulfill its duties.

The maximum duration of time that an individual can serve *(Congressional term limits)* in the House of Representatives shall be no longer than twenty years. Individuals who are presently serving in the Congress of the United States who have exceeded the limit of twenty years can continue to serve for the three-year transition period but cannot continue or be reelected to the new Congress. They must retire after the three-year transition period ends.

The act of filibustering, or any other act by members of the House of Representatives designed to delay a vote, is not allowed in the procedures of House of Representatives.

Members of the House of Representatives have a right to have their bills given a vote by the full House. Any bill submitted by a member of the House of Representatives shall be delayed no longer than one year after formal submittal. After one year has lapsed, the bill must be submitted for a vote by the full House of Representatives. The bill may be amended in committee but must be submitted for a vote after one year from its original submittal. Neither spending amendments nor riders that are not directly related to the original intent of a bill shall be added to any bill. *(This last sentence is aimed directly at the issue of earmarks.)*

No member of Congress shall cast a vote for another member for any reason whatsoever.

No initiative will be undertaken that prevents a vote on a bill, such as but not limited to the "Self-Extracting Rule," more commonly known as the "Deem & Pass Rule."

The Vice President shall be the President of the House of Representatives, but shall have no vote unless there is a tie vote due to a member or members not being present or otherwise unable to vote.

No member of the House of Representatives can abstain on a vote, but must vote for or against it.

This section sets the size of the House, apportioned according to the population census, and sets term limits for the representatives. The odd number of representatives means that there will not be a tie vote.

I have inserted the second paragraph here that defines how exactly congressional districts are to be determined as a way to eliminate gerrymandering. The dividing up of a state along arbitrary boundaries for the political advantage of one political party is an affront to the democratic principle, if not a step toward the dictatorship of one party.

The third paragraph is the only time I have placed a mandate upon the states as to their organization. By stipulating that the state legislatures must conform to the county border concept for the determination of representatives to the state legislature, gerrymandering will also be eliminated on the state level. State county borders should not be changed as a back-door method to get around this.

The fourth paragraph includes a specific means for the replacement of a representative, in order to prevent what has been seen in recent times, which is the deliberate changing of state law for political advantage. In that respect, I have taken the temptation for changing the method of succession away from the back-room state crowd and set it in concrete here.

The present situation where an individual can remain in Congress indefinitely leads to a new American royalty class who feel they are entitled to the seat in Congress and who therefore engage in activities designed to get them reelected instead of working on the affairs of the country. With the present membership increased from 435 to 499, the number of representatives per state should go up. Hopefully, it will allow for more interaction between the representatives and their constituents.

I have removed the ability of one or more members of the House to delay a vote. I feel that this action of delaying a vote is nothing more than an adult temper tantrum and interferes with the affairs of the nation. We are, after all, a democracy, and the majority will should prevail. Delay of the will of the majority is not democracy.

Presently, if a bill is submitted by a member of the House, the leadership can hold this bill up from ever getting to committee or getting to the floor for a vote. I feel that this is patently unfair. I believe that every member of the House has a right to have his or her bill debated in committee and voted on by the full House. We voters send these people to Congress to do a job, and it is undemocratic—if not outright unfair— to have a few members of the congressional leadership circumvent the will of the people who sent their representative to Washington. To do otherwise is nothing more than setting up a new royalty class who decides for all of us. This is not democracy.

I have banned the "Self-Extracting Rule." This way of passing a bill without having members of Congress stand up and be counted is something that was being talked about as a way to pass the Health Care bill on the sly. I believe this sneaky process is inherently wrong.

The Vice President is now President of the Senate, but I have made the Vice President the President of the House of Representatives instead. The Vice President shall have a vote only when there is a tie due to the absence of a member or members of the House.

Most of what is in Section 3 here was included in Section 2 and Section 3 of the original Constitution. Because of the changes, I feel it is clearer to have a different section. The original Constitution goes into the organization of the House and Senate; however, since I have eliminated the Senate, these sections can be combined and slimmed down. Mention of taxes is removed and inserted into Section 10, and mention of impeachment is included in Section 4.

Section 4: The House of Representatives shall have the power of impeachment. A majority vote is required to impeach a federal official. Once an official has been impeached by the House, he or she is disallowed from exercising any official duties until proven innocent by the Supreme Court.

If the President of the United States is so impeached, the Vice President shall assume the presidential duties until the President is proven innocent by the Supreme Court, whereupon the President shall resume his duties.

If the Vice President is impeached, the President shall appoint an individual to act in his place temporarily until the Vice President is proven innocent by the Supreme Court.

The Supreme Court shall have the power to try all impeachments. A majority vote of eight Supreme Court justices is needed to remove an official from office. Judgment of the Supreme Court on impeachment shall extend no further than removal from office and disqualification to hold any office of honor, trust, or profit under the United States, which includes lobbying members of the United States government. The party so convicted by the Supreme Court shall nevertheless be liable and subject to indictment, trial, judgment, and punishment according to the law.

There is no appeal of the Supreme Court's decision on impeachment unless there is new evidence that may cause the Supreme Court to overturn its previous decision. If such a decision is overturned, and sufficient time has elapsed that a permanent replacement has been made to the defendant's former federal position, the position is not to be regained, but the reputation of the official shall become untarnished.

We have seen, in recent history, that the impeachment process has become too politicized. Moving the trial from the legislature to the Supreme Court eliminates this.

Section 5: The place and manner of holding elections for the President, Vice President, and members of the House of Representatives shall be prescribed in each state by the legislatures thereof, but the duration of the election campaign shall be no longer than four months. A simple majority vote of those votes cast shall be needed for election to federal office. The President and Vice President shall run together, from the same political party, and voting shall be for the pair.

Polling places for Presidential, Vice Presidential, and congressional elections shall be open from 5 AM to 10 PM on Election Day.

The right of citizens of the United States, who are eighteen years of age or older, to vote in any primary or other election for President or Vice President, Members of the Congress, or members of state government, shall not be denied or abridged by the United States or any state by reason of failure to pay any poll tax or other tax. *(The voting age requirement is originally from the twenty-sixth amendment. The unlawful use of a poll tax is the twenty-fourth amendment of the original Constitution.)*

News media is expressly forbidden from announcing any election results until the last election polling places closes in the United States.

The election for President, Vice President, and members of the House of Representatives shall be held on the first Saturday of April.

The terms of office of President, Vice President, and members of the House of Representatives shall begin and end at noon on the first Saturday in June of the years when an election is held.

The Congress shall assemble at least once a year, and such meeting shall be on the second Monday in June.

The long election campaigns have become a media circus, and restricting the duration of the official campaign to four months will reduce this, as well as hopefully restrict the excessive spending on these campaigns. This may open up the election process so that more people will feel that they can run for Congress.

The restriction on the news media is the only restriction in this constitution, and it is intended to prevent undue influence on the electorate in the Western states by forecasting a winner based on early—if not skimpy—exit poling results from the Eastern states. It also makes the electorate in the Western states feel that their vote is worth something in that their vote has not been made irreverent by the news media or manipulated by them. We have also seen announcements of a projected winner when only the results of a few states are in. This is ridiculous and designed only to garner ratings for the TV media.

I have moved the election date to a time of the year when the weather will be milder, which should allow more people to get out and vote. Additionally, by holding the elections on a Saturday, more people will be off from work and therefore able to get to vote.

Section 6: *(Death of the President or Vice President)*

If, at the time fixed for the beginning of the term of President, the President-elect shall have died, the Vice President-elect shall become President.

In case of the removal of the President from office or of his death or resignation, the Vice President shall become President.

If, at the time fixed for the beginning of the term of the Vice President, the Vice President-elect shall have died, the President-elect shall nominate a Vice President-elect who shall take the office of Vice President-elect upon confirmation by a majority vote of the Congress, or if insufficient time is available to nominate a Vice President-elect, then after the President-elect takes the office of President, his nominee shall be confirmed by a majority vote of the Congress, whereupon the nominee will take the office of Vice President.

Whenever there is a vacancy in the office of the Vice President, the President shall nominate a Vice President who shall take the office upon confirmation by a majority vote of the Congress.

Whenever the President transmits to the Speaker of the House of Representatives his written declaration that he is unable to discharge the powers and duties of his office, and until he transmits to them a written declaration to the contrary, such powers and duties shall be discharged by the Vice President as acting President.

Whenever the Vice President and a majority of either the principal officers of the executive departments or the President's cabinet transmit to the speaker of the House of Representatives their written declaration that the President is unable to discharge the powers and duties of his office, the Vice President shall immediately assume the powers and duties of the office as acting President.

Thereafter, when the President transmits to the Speaker of the House of Representatives his written declaration that no inability exists, he shall resume the powers and duties of his office, unless the Vice President and a majority of either the principal officers of the executive departments or the President's cabinet transmit within four days to the speaker of the House of Representatives their written declaration that the President is unable to discharge the powers and duties of his office. Thereupon, Congress shall decide the issue, assembling within forty-eight hours for that purpose if not in session. If the Congress within twenty-one days after receipt of the latter declaration or, if Congress is not in session, within twenty-one days after Congress is required to assemble, determines by a two-thirds vote that the President is unable to discharge the powers and duties of his office, the Vice President shall continue to discharge the same as acting President; otherwise, the President shall resume the powers and duties of his office.

In these sections, items from the twenty-fifth amendment are used, along with my own construction of presidential and vice presidential succession or disability, to define this issue more precisely.

If the unfortunate circumstance occurs where both the President-elect and the Vice President-elect both die before assuming their offices, then the outgoing President and Vice President shall continue in office for a period of time not to exceed one year. There is to be a new election within this one-year period for the people to select a new President and Vice President. ** *(Much of this is extracted from the twenty-fifth amendment and placed here where the issue of elections is discussed.)*

If a President-elect before beginning his term is shown to be unqualified, then the Vice President-elect shall act as President until the President-elect becomes qualified. In the event the President-elect fails to qualify, then the Vice President shall become the President.

If a Vice President-elect before beginning his term is shown to be unqualified, then the President-elect shall nominate a Vice President-elect who shall take the office of Vice President-elect upon confirmation by a majority vote of the Congress. If insufficient time is available to nominate a Vice President-elect, then after the President elect takes the office of President, his nominee shall be confirmed by a majority vote of the Congress, whereupon the nominee will take the office of vice President.

In the case wherein neither a President-elect nor the Vice President-elect shall have been shown to be qualified, the Congress shall vote to declare the election results null and void by a majority vote. Then the outgoing President and Vice President shall continue in office for a period of time not to exceed one year. There is to be a new election within this one-year period for the people to select a new President and Vice President.

The Congress of the United States shall make laws regarding election fraud, defined as casting more than one election ballet or modifying or destroying election ballots, as a capital offense punishable according to the laws that they in act.

The method of succession is presently spread between the initial Constitution and the Bill of Rights, and it appears to be a mish mash of ideas. I have clarified the process here and have included conditions that have been overlooked in the existing constitution.

Subversion of the "one man one vote" principle should be considered right up there with treason as an attempt to undermine our democratic ideals, and a severe punishment, determined by Congress, should be applied.

Section *7:* The House of Representatives shall be the judge of the elections, returns, and qualifications of its own members, and a majority shall constitute quorum to do business; but, a smaller number may adjourn from day to day and are authorized to compel the attendance of absent members, in such a manner and under such penalties as the House may provide.

The House may determine the rules of its proceedings, punish its members for disorderly behavior, and with the concurrence of two-thirds expel a member.

The House of Representatives shall keep a journal of its proceedings and from time to time publish the same, excepting such parts as may in their judgment require secrecy, and the yeas and nays of the members are to be entered into the proceedings.

Section 7 here was included within Section 5 of the original Constitution. The third paragraph mandates that the voting record of the House members be noted in the proceedings and become a matter of public record.

Section *8:* The members of the House of Representatives shall receive a compensation for their services, to be ascertained by law, and paid out of the Treasury of the United States. They shall in all cases, except treason, felony, breach of the peace, or abuse of mind-altering substances such as drugs or alcohol, be privileged from arrest during their attendance at the session of the House, as well as in going to and returning from the same, and for any speech or debate in the House, they shall not be questioned in any other place.

Whenever a member of the House of Representatives is subject to a legal proceeding, these proceedings cannot be closed nor sequestered but must be open to public scrutiny and review.

No member of the House of Representatives shall, during the time for which they were elected, be appointed to any civil office under the authority of the United States, which shall have been created or the emoluments whereof shall have been increased during such time, and no person holding any office under the United States shall be a member of the House of Representatives.

This section was included within Section 6 of the original Constitution. The only new thing here is that I allow a Congressman to be arrested for using drugs or alcohol to excess if the law feels that his or her behavior outside of Congress warrants an arrest. We have all seen alcohol used to excess, and driving while impaired due to alcohol or drugs should not be condoned nor should Congressmen be absolved from punishment from driving drunk or impairment from the use of drugs. We elected them to represent us; however, in doing so, we did not give them license to kill us on the highways. The people who elected their Congressman have a right to know if the person they sent to Washington is behaving in a decent manner.

Additionally, the requirement has been added that any legal proceedings of a Congressional member not to be secret but must be open for public review. We are reminded about a certain Massachusetts Senator who drove his car off a bridge, killing a staff member. The proceedings were not open to public scrutiny, and they should have been. Political influence prevailed here. The people have a right to know about their representatives' behavior, embarrassment or political consequences be damned. To do so otherwise is nothing more than establishing a privileged class that can get away with anything.

Section 9: Every bill that has passed the House of Representatives shall, before it becomes law, be presented to the President of the United States. If he approves, he shall sign it, and it will become law, but if not, he shall return it with his objections to the House of Representatives. The objections shall be entered into the House journal, and the House shall proceed to reconsider these objections. If, after such reconsideration, two-thirds of the House agrees to pass the bill, it shall become law over the objections of the President. If any bill shall not be returned by the President within ten days (Sundays excepted) after it shall have been presented to him, the same shall be a law, in like manner as if he had signed it, unless the Congress by their adjournment prevents its return, in which case it shall not be a law.

Every order and resolution of vote to which the concurrence of the House may be necessary (except on a question of adjournment) shall be presented to the President of the United States, and before the same shall take effect, it shall be approved by him, or being disproved by him, it shall be re-passed by two-thirds of the House according to the rules and limitations prescribed in the case of the bill.

No changes here over the present Constitution except for the elimination of references to the Senate. These issues are found in Section 7 of the original Constitution.

Section 10: The Congress shall have the power to collect revenue through one tax upon the people of the United States only, and that tax shall be a flat rate individual income tax, not to exceed 20% of a person's income, with no exemptions, deductions, credits, or adjustments to income allowed. These revenues shall be used to provide for a common defense and general operation of the United States government only. At the conclusion of the transition period for adopting this constitution, all other federal taxes in existence shall become null and void.

The word "only" is used here to prevent the distribution of federal funds to the states. It sounds like I'm being mean. All too often we have seen state governors/politicians hit up the federal government in an attempt to bail them out of making difficult financial decisions. This is nothing less than financial incompetence on the state's part. If the states need money for state projects, then they should raise it within their own state, and the citizens of that state should pay for it. It is not right for someone in one state to pay for something in another state. I do, however, make up for part of this with the following proviso.

The Congress shall have the power to impose tariffs, as necessary, on international trade.

The Congress of the United States shall pass no unfunded mandates upon the states, and any mandate placed upon the states by the government of the United States shall include the financial resources to carry out the mandate.

The budget of the United States shall be in balance every calendar year in that the government shall not spend more money than it takes in. The government is granted the right to borrow money on the credit of the United States, provided such borrowing stays within balance over the long term. The only exception allowed is when there is a declared state of war, and additional revenues are needed to prosecute the war. In so doing, the Congress may borrow funds needed and spend in an unbalanced way. At the conclusion of hostilities, the borrowed funds shall be repaid over a twenty-year period. If the Congress fails in its duty to repay war debts, then the President of the United States is required by Presidential order to the Treasury Department to schedule and authorize payment over Congressional objections.

The authority to coin and print money, and regulate its value, is relegated to the Congress of the United States, and the government of the United States is the only recognized authority allowed to do so. The Congress shall provide for the punishment of counterfeiting the currency and securities of the United States.

The currency of the United States shall be a two-tier system with one design of currency for use within the states and another for use outside the United States. The currency designed for use within the United States, if taken outside the United States, is not to be accepted back into the country. Exchange of currency is to take place within the United States through the banking system, and records are to be kept as to who is exchanging this money. Currency designed for use outside the United States can be brought into the country and exchanged through the banking system inside the United States. Currency designed for use outside the United States is not allowed to be used for transactions within the United States, and currency designed for use within the United States is not allowed to be used for transactions outside the United States.

Adoption of the two-tier currency system is to take place four years from the date of adoption of this constitution. The Treasury department shall design new currency to be used both inside and outside the United States. From the beginning of year three after adoption of this constitution, currency both inside and outside the United States is to be exchanged into new currency. One year will be allotted for this. Present currency in circulation beginning year four after adoption of this constitution is to be worthless.

The authority to raise revenue is mentioned in Section 7 of the original Constitution. I have authorized the government one and only one means to collect revenue from the people, through a flat tax. Over time the government has burdened its people with additional taxes and fees, which are becoming too heavy and burdensome to bear, in an attempt to raise additional revenue to satisfy Congress's urge to spend. The situation has become ridiculous and beyond reason. The tax code is a mess. The first and second paragraphs of Section 10 set into concrete that the Congress is allowed only one means to raise revenue from the people and must live within the limits that this imposes. The only other means of raising revenue allowed is through tariffs. Some might argue that I have tied the hands of Congress to raise funds. I agree wholeheartedly that unrestrained spending and the national debt that it shackles our people with represent a new kind of tyranny. This debt tyranny will ultimately lead to our downfall as a nation. The first commandment for politicians will now be as follows: "You shall balance your budget."

It also might seem harsh that I stipulate that "no exemptions, deductions, credits or adjustments to income [are] allowed." *The tax code has become riddled with so many holes that it has essentially become more unfair than fair. This stipulation will simplify the tax process, making the tax form printable on just one side of a piece of paper. On the whole, many people escaping taxes now will not in the future. As to the argument that it is unfair to working families, I disagree.*

The second paragraph should make a lot of state governors happy, as the federal government has burdened the states with unfunded mandates throwing their budgets into disarray. It makes common sense that, if the federal government is going to mandate that a state do something, it provides the money to do it. Presently, the Congress gets away with providing benefits and looking good without providing the money for it, putting the burden on the backs of the states and their taxpayers.

The third paragraph of this section mandates a balanced budget. This is some-

thing we do not have now, and it should have been included in the original Constitution but wasn't—probably because it was inconceivable to the original framers of the Constitution that the budget would not be in balance. The exception noted for a balanced budget is in case of a declared state of war. The debts incurred by the government to prosecute the war are to be paid back over a twenty-year period. I also stipulate that, if the Congress fails in its duty to repay the debt, the President has the means to repay it over the objections of the Congress. This is the only time the Congress can be overruled by the President.

The two-tier currency system is specifically designed to crimp two types of illegal activity: the drug trade and international counterfeiting of United States currency. By preventing large sums of United States currency designed for use within the borders of the United States from moving across the border, it will be impossible for drug traders from repatriating their ill-gotten gains. The exchange of so much money into the currency designed for use outside the United States will not go unnoticed by law enforcement authorities. The counterfeiting of currency designed for use inside the United States by foreign entities will be of no use to them, as this currency will not be accepted by the banking system for exchange. They could only counterfeit the currency designed for use outside the United States; however, such an attack upon the value of the external dollar will not threaten the domestic dollar value.

Section 11: It is no longer recognized that the government of the United States should keep and operate a post office. The existing post office department of the United States government at the time of adoption of this constitution is to be sold and made a public corporation; however, such a sale should be done with the proviso that daily home and business delivery service will be maintained.

The authorization for a post office is in Section 8 of the original Constitution. With so many competing delivery companies, such as Federal Express, UPS, etc., it makes no sense for the government to maintain a post office. In colonial times, the government was the only authority that could possibly start up and operate such a venture, but now government operation of a post office is no longer justified. It also is losing money and is a drag on tax dollars better used elsewhere.

Section 12: The following powers are granted to the Congress of the United States:

To regulate commerce with foreign nations, and among the states and with Indian tribes.

To establish a uniform rule of naturalization. Children born to non-citizens of the United States, while in the United States, however, are to be considered citizens of the nation of the parents and are not automatically to be granted citizenship of the United States because they were born here.

To promote the progress of science and the useful arts by securing for a limited time for authors and inventors the exclusive rights to their respective writings and discoveries (*i.e.*, *patents*). When according to government regulation a discovery must be tested for an extended time, the length of this test time is to be added to the patent duration established by Congress.

To establish uniform laws on the subject to bankruptcies throughout the United States. The concept that a corporation is too big to fail is rejected by this constitution. The Congress shall enact appropriate legislation for corporate and investment regulation, plus legislation for the orderly dissolution of companies that become financially insolvent. The people's money is not to be used to rescue insolvent corporations.

To fix the standard of weights and measures for the Unites States according to the metric system and set the established temperature standard as the Kelvin scale. The time standard for the United States shall be standard time year round. The process known as daylight saving time is no longer allowed.

To constitute tribunals inferior to the Supreme Court.

To define and punish piracies and felonies committed on the high seas and offenses against the laws of nations.

To declare war. The President of the United States is to be considered the Commander in Chief of the United States military and has the authority to use the military to defend the United States for a period of time not to exceed sixty days. After that time, if the Congress has not declared that a state of war exists, then the military action authorized by the President is to cease.

To raise and support the United States military.

To raise and support a coast guard for the maintenance and navigation of the nations waterways.

To make rules for the government and regulation of the United States military and coast guard.

To provide for the calling forth of the states' militia to execute the laws of the nation and to defend the union.

To provide for the organizing, arming, and disciplining of the militia and for governing such part of them as may be employed in the service of the United States, reserving to the states respectively the appointment of the officers and authority of training the militia according to the discipline prescribed by Congress.

To exercise exclusive legislation in all cases whatsoever, over those lands managed by the Federal Government, such as but not limited to military bases, ship yards, arsenals, national parks, and wilderness areas.

To make all laws which shall be necessary and proper for carrying into execution the forgoing powers, and all other powers vested by this constitution in the government of the United States or in any department of officer thereof.

Most of what is in Section 11 here is extracted from Article 1, Section 8 and Section

9 of the original Constitution. Some new issues are presented here. One is to oppose the "anchor baby" concept, in that, if an infant is born in the United States to non-citizen parents, he or she is not automatically granted United States citizenship. This is to prevent people from coming across the border to have their children, thinking that they cannot be forced back to their nation of origin.

Another is the idea that, if a company develops a product that is required by government regulation to be tested, test time should be added to the duration of the patent. This seems only fair since some required testing could take years. It makes no sense for a company to have a product's commercial viability reduced by government-required test time.

Given recent events, I have inserted a stipulation against the use of the people's money to bail out insolvent corporations. The constitutionally recognized concept that a corporation is not too big to fail is vital in the management of our economy. If the Congress had not been asleep at the controls of the economy, if appropriate regulation had been in force, and if the Glass Steagall Act had not been rescinded, the financial calamity we are going through probably would not have occurred.

The requirements that the metric standard be adopted as the official standard of weights and measures and the adoption of the Kelvin temperature scale may cause quite a stir. It is time for the United States to get off this antiquated foot and mile standard and join the rest of the world using the metric system. The Kelvin scale has an advantage over either the Fahrenheit or the Centigrade scale in that absolute zero is absolute zero. The freezing point of water is 273 deg. K and the boiling pint of water is 373 deg. K. In both the Fahrenheit and Centigrade scales, the zero point is arbitrarily located.

I have always hated the change in clocks that put us into and out of daylight saving time. The adoption of standard time year round is a personal issue of mine. Writing this constitution gives me the opportunity to mandate standard time as the official time standard year round.

The last is the Presidential authorization to use the military no longer than sixty days without the consent of Congress. If so used, these forces must stand down after the sixty-day period if Congress does not declare war.

Old references to Armies, the Navy, letters of Marque and Reprisal, etc., are done away with.

Section 13: The territory known as the "District of Columbia" presently governed by the Congress of the United States is to be divided between the states of Maryland and Virginia. The portion of the District of Columbia that is east of the Potomac River is to be included within the State of Maryland and will be known as the city of Washington. The portion that is west of the Potomac River is to be included within the State of Virginia. Those buildings and lands used by the United States government in the District of Columbia shall remain under the control of the Congress of the United States. If in the future it is determined that any of these buildings and lands in the district presently used by the United States are to be declared surplus, then they are to be surrendered to the state within which they reside to be disposed of as the state determines.

The division of the District of Columbia wherein the city of Washington resides is to be divided over a three-year period after adoption of this constitution. The population of the respective two parts is to be included within the states of Maryland and Virginia for determination of congressional districts.

The Congress of the United States shall provide financial remuneration to the local municipalities for the civil services that are required for the operation of the United States government facilities within these municipalities.

The issue of the District of Columbia is mentioned in Section 8 of the original Constitution. The concept of a special district, I believe, should be done away with. I see no reason for the city of Washington D.C. to not be included within the states of Maryland and Virginia. Additionally, I have provided compensation to city government for the costs of supporting federal facilities within the cities of this nation.

Section 14: The privilege of the Writ of Habeas Corpus shall not be suspended, unless when in cases of rebellion or invasion public safety may require it.

No bill of attainder or ex post facto law shall be passed.

No tax or duty shall be laid on articles exported in trade between the states.

No preference shall be given to any Regulation of Commerce or Revenue to the ports of one state over those of another, nor shall commercial transportation bound to, or from, one state be obligated to enter, clear, or pay duties in another.

No money shall be drawn from the Treasury, but in consequence of Appropriations made by law, and a regular statement and account of the receipts and expenditures of all public money shall be published from time to time.

No title of nobility shall be granted by the United States. And no person holding any office of profit or trust under them shall without the consent of the Congress accept of any present, emolument, office, or title, of any kind whatever, from any King, Prince, or foreign state.

The right of citizens of the United States to vote shall not be denied or abridged by the United States or by any State on account of race, color, sex, or previous conditions of servitude.

Most of what is found here is in Section 9 of the original Constitution. The first paragraph of Section 9 that allows the importation of slaves is obviously eliminated. The last item combines portions of the fifteenth and nineteenth amendments.

Section 15: No state shall enter into any treaty, alliance or confederation;

coin or print money; pass any bill of attainder, ex post facto law, or law impairing the obligations of contracts; or grant any title of nobility.

No state shall, without the consent of the Congress, lay any imposts or duties on imports or exports, except what may be absolutely necessary for executing its inspection laws, nor lay any duty of tonnage. The net produce of all duties and imposts laid by any state on imports or exports shall be for the use of the Treasury of the United States, and all such laws shall be subject t the revision and control of the Congress.

No state shall, without the consent of Congress, enter into any military agreement with another state or a foreign power, or engage in war, unless actually invaded or in such imminent danger as will not admit delay.

Most of what is here is found in Article 1, Section 10 of the original Constitution.

Section 16: The Congress shall pass a set of ethics codes for its members to follow. These codes shall also stipulate mandated punishments for violations of the codes.

Section 17: All Federal lands under the control of the Federal Government at the time of the incorporation of this constitution, except those lands directly needed for the operation of governmental functions, are to be surrendered to the sovereignty of the individual states wherein they reside. Congressional control of these lands will end with acceptance of this constitution.

The Federal government owns vast swaths of land in the West. It is my feeling that these lands should not belong to the Federal government but to the states. This Section clarifies that these lands are to be surrendered to the states.

Article 2
Section 1: The executive power shall be vested in a President of the United States of America. The president shall hold office during the term of four years, and, together with the Vice President, chosen for the same term, be elected by majority popular vote of the people.

The method of electing the President and Vice President prescribed in the existing Constitution via an electoral college is done away with here. The rational for an electoral college used during the time of the framing of the existing Constitution no longer applies.

No person except a natural-born citizen, who has been born within the borders of the United States, or a person born within the territories of the United States, at the time of the adoption of this constitution, shall be eligible for the office of President or Vice President; neither shall any person be eligible for these offices who shall not have attained the age of thirty-five years.

Candidates for the office of President and Vice President shall, at the time of their announcement to run for office, provide public proof that they indeed comply with the natural-born citizenship requirement.

The president shall, at stated times, receive for his services a compensation, which shall neither be increased nor decreased during the period for which he shall have been elected, and he shall not receive within the period any other emolument from the United States.

Before the President enters on the execution of his office, he shall take the following oath or affirmation: "I, (Name), do solemnly swear (or affirm) that I will faithfully execute the office of President of the United States, and will, to the best of my ability, preserve, protect, and defend the constitution of the United States."

No person shall be elected to the office of the President more than twice, and no person who has held the office of President, or acted as President, for more than two years of a term to which some other person was elected President shall be elected to the office of the President more than once.

The entire section regarding the electors for the Presidential elections has been removed. This is found within Article 2, Section 1 of the original Constitution. The President and Vice President will now be elected by majority popular vote.

Additionally, I have inserted a proviso that candidates provide proof that they comply with the "natural-born citizen" requirement. This is intended to eliminate any further question as to a candidate's qualification for the Presidency and Vice Presidency, as has evolved for President Obama.

The last part is the twenty-second amendment, with regard to the President serving only two terms, which I have inserted here.

Section 2: The President shall be Commander in Chief of the United States military, and of the militia of the several states, when called into actual service of the United States.

The President shall have the power to grant reprieves and pardons for offenses against the United States, except in cases of impeachment.

The President shall have power, by and with the advice and consent of the Congress, to make treaties, provided two-thirds of the Congress present concurs; however, no treaty made with a foreign government shall usurp the provisions of this constitution. If a treaty is made where conflicts arise with the provisions of the constitution, the treaty is to be considered null and void.

The President shall nominate and, by and with the advice and consent of the Congress, shall appoint ambassadors, other public ministers and consuls, judges of the Supreme Court, and all other officers of the United States, whose appointments are not herein otherwise provided for and which shall be established by law. The Congress may by law vest the appointments of such inferior officers, as they think proper, in the President alone, in the courts of law, or in the heads of departments.

When the President makes an appointment that requires congressional approval, the Congress has three months to act on the nomination, and if the Congress fails to approve or disapprove the nomination, the nomination is to be considered approved.

The President shall have the power to fill up all vacancies that may happen during the recess of the **Congress**, by granting commissions that shall expire at the end of their next session.

The above comes from of Article 2, Section 2 of the original Constitution with some minor changes. Due to the possibility of a treaty with a foreign government or organization either intentionally or unintentionally seeming to circumvent the provisions of this constitution, the requirement that no treaty usurping the provisions of the constitution is allowed has been inserted here.

We have seen political football with presidential appointments not being approved by Congress for partisan political reasons, despite the qualifications of the appointee. This is true for judgeships and many other positions. The provision with regard to presidential appointments being approved if Congress takes no action on them is to stop the practice of doing nothing on presidential appointments. This will force congressional action on these appointees.

Section 3: The President shall from time to time give to the Congress information as to the state of the Union and recommend to their consideration such measures as the President shall judge necessary and expedient.

The President may, on extraordinary occasions, convene the **Congress**, and in case of disagreement between them, with respect to the time of adjournment, he may adjourn them to such time as he shall think proper.

The President shall receive ambassadors and other public ministers; he shall take care that the laws be faithfully executed and shall commission all officers of the United States.

The above comes from Article 2, Section 3 of the original Constitution with minor changes. I tried to think of ways to stop the State of the Union speech from becoming a political pep rally, but just couldn't think of the words.

Section 4: The President, Vice President, and all civil officers of the United States shall be removed from office on impeachment for and conviction of treason, bribery, or other high crimes and misdemeanors.
The above comes from Article 2, Section 4 of the original Constitution with no change.

Section 5: The President of the United States shall be briefed on the operational and financial status of all classified programs run by agencies of the

United States government, and shall have full authority to start, continue to run or terminate any program. The president is also authorized to make public any program the president deems necessary for the public's benefit.

Article 3

Section 1: The judicial power of the United States shall be vested in one Supreme Court and in such inferior courts as the Congress may from time to time ordain and establish. The judges, both of the Supreme Court and inferior courts, shall hold their offices during good behavior for a period of time not to exceed fifteen years, and shall, at stated times, receive for their services a compensation, which shall not be diminished during their continuance in office.

There shall be nine justices on the Supreme Court appointed by the President and approved my majority vote of the Congress.

The above comes from Article 3, Section 1 of the original Constitution with one change. I have inserted a term limit for the Supreme Court justices of fifteen years. Given that in recent history, we have seen judges elevated to the Supreme Court in mid-life and serve until they are doddering old people, I think it prudent to limit the time served on the Supreme Court. The country should have justices sharp in mind and body on the bench. Additionally, the number of justices is fixed by this Section, as well as how they get appointed and who approves them to serve.

Section 2: The judicial power shall extend to all cases, in law and equity, arising under this constitution, the laws of the United States, and treaties made, or which shall be made, under their authority; to all cases affecting ambassadors, other public ministers, and consuls; to all cases admiralty and maritime jurisdictions; to controversies to which the United States shall be a party; to controversies between two or more states, between citizens of different states, between citizens of the same state claiming lands under grant of different states and between a state, or the citizens thereof, and foreign states, citizens, or subjects.

The judicial power of the United States shall not be construed to extend to any suit in law or equity commenced or prosecuted against on the United States by citizens of another state, or by citizens or subjects of any foreign state. *(This is the eleventh amendment.)*

In all cases affecting ambassadors, other public ministers and consuls, and those in which a state shall be a party, the Supreme Court shall have original jurisdiction. In all the other cases before mentioned, the Supreme Court shall have appellate jurisdiction, both as to law and fact, with such exceptions and under such regulations as the Congress shall make.

The trial of all crimes, except in cases of Impeachment, shall be by jury, and such trial shall be held in the state where the said crimes shall have been committed; but when not committed within any state, the trial shall be at such place or places as the Congress may by law have directed.

The above comes from Article 3, Section 2 of the original Constitution with no change, except for the insertion of the eleventh amendment of the original Constitution, which considered the issue of cases "between a state and citizens of another state."

Section 3: Treason against the United States shall consist of only levying war against the United States, or adhering to our enemies, giving them aid and comfort. No person shall be convicted of treason less on the testimony of two witnesses to the same avert act, on confession in open court, or on the presentation of overwhelming evidence.

The above comes from Article 3, Section 3 of the original Constitution with no change, except for the insertion of "overwhelming evidence." Given changes in criminal investigating techniques since the original framing of the Constitution, it is considered relevant to include "evidence," which can be just as damning as eyewitness testimony, if not more so.

Section 4: The punishment for treason shall be death, and the death penalty shall be recognized as a lawful punishment for the crimes of treason, premeditated murder, kidnapping, carjacking, or acts of terrorism where there is injury, loss of life, or destruction of property when weapons such as firearms, explosives, chemicals, poison gas, or if biological agents are used. If in the opinion of the court, a lesser punishment is warranted, due to circumstances of the case, a prison sentence can be declared.

The accepted method of execution shall be either death by gas chamber or by lethal injection, as defined by Congress or the individual states.

The above section is new. I thought it necessary to define the punishment for the mentioned crimes in that the death penalty is a recognized and accepted form of punishment. I also thought it necessary to define exactly what method of execution would be accepted.

Section 5: The Chief Justice of the Supreme Court shall appoint a five-member standing committee whose responsibility will be to investigate ethics violations of members of the House of Representatives. The investigation shall determine if the Congressional ethics codes have been violated. Recommendations from the committee shall be voted on by the Supreme Court, and a vote of eight justices will be required to accept the committee's recommendations. The recommendations shall extend no further than a Supreme Court order that the Congress consider a motion of impeachment against its members; however, lesser penalties, as stipulated by the Congressional ethics codes, can be ordered by the Supreme Court for minor ethics infractions. If a motion for impeachment is so issued by the Supreme Court, it cannot be ignored by the House of

Representatives. If the House of Representatives chooses to ignore an impeachment order, then the Chief Justice of the Supreme Court is authorized to order the Attorney General to remove the member of Congress in question from all federal facilities and keep the member so removed. The committee is given power to subpoena evidence and compel testimony by this constitution.

Having the Congress police itself on ethics charges has been prone to the old boys' school of self-protection of its members. We have all seen members charged with an ethics offense and get away with a slap on the wrist. This way, an independent committee will have power to investigate an ethics offense and recommend punishment.

Article 4

Section 1: Full faith and credit shall be given in each state to the public acts, records, and judicial proceedings of every other state. And the Congress may by general laws prescribe the manner in which such acts, records, and proceedings shall be proved, and the effect thereof.

No change from the original Constitution.

Section 2: The citizens of each state shall be entitled to all privileges and immunities of citizens in several states.

A person charged in any state with treason, felony, or other crime who shall flee from justice and be found in another state shall on demand of the executive authority of the state from which he fled be delivered up, to be removed to the state having jurisdiction of the crime.

No change from the original constitution.

Neither slavery nor involuntary servitude, except as a punishment for crime whereof the party shall have been duly convicted, shall exist within the United States or in any place subject to its jurisdiction.

This paragraph is the thirteenth amendment of the original Constitution. It replaces a paragraph in the original Constitution that calls for the return of escaped slaves.

Section 3: New states may be admitted by Congress into the union, but no new state shall be formed or erected within the jurisdiction of any other state—nor any state be formed by the junction of two or more states, or parts of states—without the consent of the legislature of the states concerned, as well as of the Congress.

The Congress shall have power to dispose of and make all needful rules and regulations respecting the territory or other property belonging to the

United States, and nothing in this constitution shall be so construed as to prejudice any claims of the United States or of any particular state.

No change from the original Constitution.

Section 4: The United States shall guarantee to every state in this union a republican form of government, and shall protect each of them against invasion, on application of the legislature, or of the executive (when the legislature cannot be convened), against domestic violence.

No change from the original Constitution.

Article 5
Section 1: The Congress, whenever two-thirds of the representatives agree, shall approve amendments to this constitution. On the application of the legislatures of two-thirds of the several states, the Congress shall call a convention for proposing amendments, which, in either case, shall be valid to all intents and purposes as part of this constitution, when ratified by legislatures of three-fourths of the several states, or by conventions in three-fourths thereof.

The conventions when convened shall be for the purpose of debating and approving the amendment initially presented, and no other amendments are to be considered.

The first paragraph is mostly of the wording as found in the original Constitution. The second paragraph is added here to clarify that, if a convention is called, it must concern itself with only the amendment that was initially considered by the state legislatures. It must not be turned into a general discussion (free-for-all) of unrelated items not voted on by the state legislatures.

Article 6
Section 1: All debts contracted and engagements entered into before the adoption of this constitution shall be as valid against the United States under this constitution. *(This is the same wording as the existing Constitution, except I have removed reference to the Confederation.)*

This constitution and the laws of the United States which shall be made in pursuance thereof, and all treaties made, or which shall be made, under the authority of the United States, shall be the supreme law of the land, and the judges in every state shall be bound thereby any thing in the constitution or laws of any state to the contrary notwithstanding.

The members of the Congress; members of the several state legislatures; all executive and judicial officers, both of the United States and of the several states; and all members of the United States military shall be bound by oath or affirmation to support and defend this constitution, but no religious test shall ever be required as a qualification to any office or public trust under the United States. *(This is the same wording as the existing Constitution, except I have added the military to the affirmation of the constitution.)*

The first paragraph was generally conceded to be obsolete under the existing Constitution; however, it takes on a new and revised meaning with the new constitution given the debts of the federal government.

Article 7

Section 1: The approval of legislatures of three-quarters of the several states shall be sufficient for the establishment of this constitution between the states so ratifying the same.

Upon approval of this constitution, a maximum period of three years for transition will be allowed to set up the changes stated within the new constitution. Since the election for federal office has been moved to the month of April, the transition period from the time of approval of this constitution shall extend no further than the last April in the three-year period.

This article concerns itself with the approval process of this new constitution. Article 7 of the original Constitution concerned itself with ratification by nine states. Since we have more now, the wording is changed.

THE BILL OF RIGHTS

Many of the amendments in the existing Bill of Rights have been included within the new constitution. In that regard, a renumbering of the amendments would be required; however, I have kept the numbering as is for reference purposes.

Amendment One:
Congress shall make no law respecting the establishment of religion, or prohibiting the free exercise thereof, or abridging the freedom of speech, or of the press, or the right of the people to peaceable assemble, and to petition the government for a redress of grievances.

It is established that state and local aid to parochial schools is accepted provided the aid is used for the secular education of children, and not for religious instruction.

The first amendment is inserted here unchanged, but a second paragraph is added. I think it was generally understood that it was the intent of the original framers of the Constitution to set a new standard, in that the relationship between the government and the people's religious beliefs were to be none of the government's business. Where the old world nations had officially recognized state religions, in America, they would have none of this. The history of Europe is full of the intrigue and meddling between the European monarchs and the churches that have led to the inquisition of the Catholic Church, prosecution of the Jews, and outright wars between competing religious ideologies. Such conflicts even broke out in the early colonizing days in America between members of the Catholic Church and members of the Church of England. They were determined to end this nonsense, and I think the wording here establishes this. I had toyed with the idea of changing the wording to mandate that the government not establish a state religion, but thought better of it. The present wording seems to have worked fine.

I have added that it would be acceptable for states to provide aid to parochial schools, provided that the financial aid is to be used for general educational use and not used to promote the school's religious agenda. Such monies could be used for but not limited to construction, maintenance, or assistance with teacher salaries. If the parochial schools were to close within our nation's cities, the extra burden of the students then flooding into the public school system could not be assumed. The existence of parochial schools actually takes some of the tax burden off the local municipality to provide a general education.

Amendment Two:

It is recognized that the citizens of the United States have the right to self-protection, in that they have the right to keep and bear arms, and this right shall not be infringed. It is recognized that, in exercising this right, they may be required to use deadly force in protecting their persons, family, and property.

The individual states do have the right to require licenses for the carrying of concealed firearms.

The transportation of stolen firearms or ammunition, or firearms and/or ammunition smuggled into the United States, is to be a federal offense punishable according to laws enacted by Congress,

The possession of weapons of an obvious military nature, such as but not limited to fully automatic weapons, explosives, or caliber 50 weapons or larger, is not allowed. Exceptions to this are weapons older than 100 years of collector's value.

I have eliminated reference to a militia, as this issue is discussed within the constitution and need not be mentioned here. Additionally, I have stated that people have the right to self-protection, which is not mentioned in the original Amendment Two. I also clarify that, in using firearms, it is understood that the effect of this use is deadly force. The issue of state licenses is clarified here. There has been debate with regard to military-type weapons, some of which are fully automatic in their operation. I feel that these have no redeeming value for civilian self-protection and should not be allowed into general circulation.

Amendment Three:

No soldier shall, in time of peace, be quartered in any house without the consent of the owner, nor in time of war, but in a manner to be prescribed by law.

No change here from the original Constitution.

Amendment Four:

The right of the people to be secure in their persons, houses, papers, and effects against unreasonable searches and seizures shall not be violated, and no Warrants shall be issued, but upon probable cause, supported by oath or affirmation, and particularly describing the place to be searched and the persons or things to be seized.

No change here from the original Constitution.

Amendment Five:
No person shall be held to answer for a capital, of otherwise infamous, crime, unless on a presentment or indictment of a Grand Jury, except in cases arising in the **United States Military** or in the militia, when in actual service in time of war or public danger; nor shall any person be subject for the same offense be twice put in jeopardy of life and limb; nor shall be compelled in any criminal case to be a witness against himself; nor be deprived of life, liberty, or property, without due process of law; nor shall private property be taken for public use, without just compensation.

The wording is mostly the same as Amendment Five, except for the substitution of "United States Military" instead of "Land or Naval forces, or in the militia."

Amendment Six:
In all criminal prosecutions, the accused shall enjoy the right to a speedy and public trial, by an impartial jury of the state and district wherein the crime shall have been committed, which district shall have been previously ascertained by law, and to be informed of the nature and cause of the accusation, to be confronted with the witness against him, to have compulsory process for obtaining witnesses in his favor, and to have the assistance of counsel for his defense. **Individuals accused of a crime shall be considered innocent until proven guilty in a court of law.**

Upon conviction by a court of law, the convicted shall have the right to appeal, but not repeated nor multiple appeals.

The first paragraph has no change here from the original Constitution. I have inserted the proviso that an individual is innocent until proven guilty. The second paragraph is designed to eliminate the process of repeated appeals that has dragged cases through the courts for years unnecessarily.

Amendment Seven:
In suits at common law where the value in controversy shall **exceed ten thousand dollars**, the right of trial by jury shall be preserved, and no fact tried by a jury shall be otherwise re-examined in any court of the United States, then according to the rules of the common law.

I have kept the wording the same as the original amendment, except I have raised the dollar amount from twenty dollars to ten thousand. Twenty dollars may have been a lot of money in 1787, but now it would be more appropriate to raise the value and I feel ten thousand is a more appropriate value.

Amendment Eight:

Excessive bail shall not be required, nor excessive fines imposed, nor cruel and unusual punishments inflicted.

No change here from the original Constitution.

Amendment Nine:

The enumeration in the constitution of certain rights shall not be construed to deny or disparage others retained by the people.

No change here from the original Constitution.

Amendment Ten:

The powers not delegated to the United States by the constitution, nor prohibited by it to the states, are reserved to the states respectively, or to the people.

No change here from the original Constitution.

Amendment Eleven:

This has been inserted into Article 3, Section 2 of the new constitution.

Amendment Twelve:

This amendment has been made irrelevant due to the stipulation that the President and Vice President are to be elected by popular vote.

Amendment Thirteen:

The anti-slavery provision of the thirteenth amendment has been inserted into Article 4, Section 2 of this constitution.

Amendment Fourteen:
Section 1:

Item 1: *This item has been replaced by wording in Article 1, Section 11 of this constitution*

Items 2, 3, and 4: No state shall make or enforce any law that shall abridge the privileges or immunities of citizens of the United States; nor shall any state deprive any person of life, liberty, or property, without due process of law; nor deny to any person within its jurisdiction the equal protection of the law.

Section 2:
This amendment has been replaced by Article 1, Section 3 of this constitution.

Section 3:
No person who while under oath of allegiance to the United States as a government official who engaged in insurrection or rebellion against the same, or given aid and comfort to the enemies of the United States, shall hold any office within the United States government or the government of the several states.

This has been rewritten.

Section 4:
The validity of the public debt of the United States, authorized by law, shall not be questioned. But neither the United States nor any state shall assume or pay any debt or obligation incurred in aid of insurrection or rebellion against the United States.

This has been rewritten.

Section 5: The Congress shall have power to enforce, by appropriate legislation, the provisions of this article.

Amendment Fifteen:
The issue here has been included in Article 1, Section 13 of this revised constitution.

Amendment Sixteen:
This amendment is superseded by Article 1, Section 9 of this revised constitution.

Amendment Seventeen:
This amendment is superseded by Article 1, Section 1, 2, 3, etc., of this revised constitution. Since this amendment referenced the Senate and a Senate is no longer proposed in this constitution, the amendment ceases to have any validity.

Amendment Eighteen:
This was the prohibition amendment and was repealed in 1933 by the twenty-first amendment.

Amendment Nineteen:
The issue here is included in Article 1, Section 13 of this revised constitution.

Amendment Twenty:
The issue here, regarding presidential and vice presidential succession, is included in Article 1, Section 5 of this revised constitution.

28

Amendment Twenty-One:
See amendment eighteen.

Amendment Twenty-Two:
The issue here, regarding presidential term limits, is included in Article 2, Section 1 of this revised constitution

Amendment Twenty-Three:
The issue here, regarding the district constituting the seat of government, is included in Article 1, Section 12 of this revised constitution.

Amendment Twenty-Four:
The issue here, regarding poll taxes, is included in Article 1, Section 5 of this revised constitution

Amendment Twenty-Five:
The issue here, regarding presidential and vice presidential succession, is included in Article 1, Section 5 of this revised constitution.

Amendment Twenty-Six:
The issue here, regarding voting age, is included in Article 1, Section 5 of this revised constitution.

Amendment Twenty-Seven: Proposed: Entitlement Programs
Section 1: The entitlement programs known as Social Security, Medicaid, and Medicare are to be continued under this constitution; however, the Congress shall have three years from the date of enactment of this constitution to make these programs financially balanced and secure for the future. Revenues for their continuance shall continue to be extracted from paychecks as a separate deduction, as determined by Congress.

Section 2: Yearly evaluations shall be conducted by Congress to verify the continued financial viability of these programs, and adjustments made in paycheck contributions or benefits provided to secure this.

With the general recognition that these programs will become financially insolvent in the future, it is imperative that they be made financially sound. The contract made to the people of this country cannot be lightly discarded due to the financial mismanagement of the past. Promises have been made and they must be kept, but Congress will now be forced to manage the programs under a balanced budget. Congress has always kicked the can down the road with regard to stabilizing these programs. Probably they hoped that they would be out of office and the problem would be someone else's. The can cannot be kicked anymore.

Amendment Twenty-Eight: Proposed: Terrorist Tribunals
Individuals captured on a battlefield engaging in combat against forces of the United States who are not members of an established state military, whether they are citizens of the United States or not, are to be treated as prisoners of war and subject to military tribunal. Such a tribunal is to be held within a year of capture, and if it is not held within one year, the individuals so captured are to be released. If so tried by military tribunal and found guilty of waging war against the United States, the death penalty can be applied, and the method of execution shall be by military firing squad.

The purpose of this amendment is to prevent situations, as have developed recently, with regard to terrorists so captured after waging war upon the United States who have been incarcerated for long periods of time without a trial. This amendment eliminates the political failure of will to handle this situation and forces action.

Amendment Twenty-Nine: Proposed: People's Right to be Protected from Predators.
Section 1: The people of the United States have the right to go about their business free from the actions of a few that would perpetrate crimes against them. It is therefore approved by this amendment that individuals who commit crime shall be subject to a term of imprisonment of life without parole after committing three felonies or other capital crimes; however, this is left up to the individual states to impose this punishment per their state criminal codes. The Congress of the United States shall impose similar punishment standards for the commission of federal offenses.

Section 2: It is allowed by this amendment that sexual predators who commit repeated crimes are to be involuntarily castrated; however, it is left up to the individual states to amend their criminal codes to allow this.

All too often we hear stories about individuals who have rap sheets as long as your arm and are still out on the street causing mayhem in society. This amendment is intended to allow the individual states to put criminals away for life if they commit three capital offenses. In short, this is the "three time loser" law. It also makes clear that, if the states enact a "three time loser" law, it does not violate the cruel and unusual punishment proviso of this constitution.

As I write the last sentence with regard to sexual predators, there was a story on the morning news about a very pretty girl who disappeared and who was sexually assaulted by a sexual predator who had served prison time for similar crimes. It was also reported that other girls disappeared in the same area or were assaulted and got away from this guy. I cannot understand the deliberate murder after sexually assaulting a girl this pretty and believe that something has to be done that will permanently stop this from happening again. The message should be sent out that, if you behave this way in our society, then society has the right to take measures that will permanently stop you. This measure also clarifies that, if castration is done, it also does not violate the cruel and unusual punishment proviso of this constitution,

Amendment Thirty: Proposed: Corporate Taxes

Publically traded corporations are exempt from income taxes. In order to justify exempting corporations from paying income taxes, all publicly traded corporations shall be required to pay a portion of their profits in the form of a dividend to their shareholders on a quarterly or yearly basis. The only exemption allowed is when business conditions do not allow for sufficient funds to be available.

There certainly will be howls of protest that corporations should pay their fair share of income taxes; however, corporations do three basic things with their profits. They pay dividends, expand the business by buying new plants and equipment, and use them for operations. In any of these, the profits eventually go to pay people's salaries, whereupon income taxes will be paid. By eliminating the requirement for corporations to pay an income tax on their profits, they can reduce their prices and be more competitive in the global economy. This translates into more jobs for Americans. The taxes will eventually be paid through the individual income tax. As it is presently, having corporations pay income tax on their profits and then taxing individuals on the dividends paid to them is nothing short of double taxation from a greedy government. The amendment hopefully will satisfy some who feel corporations should pay income taxes.

Amendment Thirty-One: Proposed: Compulsory Purchases

The federal government shall not compel the citizens of the United States to make any purchases of any kind whatsoever.

This prohibition came directly from the Obama health care plan, where I believe it is unjust for the government to require individuals to purchase anything, including insurance.

Major Items in
This New Constitution

The major item changes in the new constitution over the existing constitution are listed here. The sections where they can be found are listed in parenthesis.

Article 1: The legislature

1. The Senate is abolished and replaced by a larger House of Representatives (Section 1).
2. Members of the House will be elected for a four-year term instead of a two-year term (Section 2).
3. The number of house members increased to 499 from 435 (Section 3).
4. The method for determining congressional and state districts is set using county borders as a way to eliminate gerrymandering (Section 3).
5. House of Representative vacancies are to be filled by appointment of the state governor. Members of immediate family are not allowed to fill the vacated seat (Section 3).
6. Term limit of twenty years is imposed for House members (Section 3).
7. Filibustering is not allowed (Section 3).
8. The House will have the power to impeach, but the trial will be held in the Supreme Court (Section 4).
9. Election campaigns are reduced to four months, and the President and Vice President are to be elected by popular vote (Section 5).
10. The election date is moved to the spring (Section 5).
11. The news media is forbidden to release election results till all polls close. Polling places are to remain open for the defined and extended period of time (Section 5).

12. Presidential and Vice Presidential succession issues are clarified (Section 6).
13. Congress has the right to tax via a flat tax only. All other federal taxes are abolished (Section 10).
14. The Congress shall pass no unfunded mandates upon the states (Section 10).
15. The United States budget is to be in balance yearly (Section 10).
16. The currency system is to be a two-tier currency system (Section 10).
17. The post office system is to be sold off and made a public company (Section 11).
18. The "anchor baby" concept for illegal immigrants is no longer recognized (Section 12).
19. The metric system is mandated as the only acceptable system of weights and measures. Standard time year round is mandated with daylight saving time disallowed (Section 12).
20. Presidential authority to use the military in hostilities is limited to sixty days (Section 12).
21. The District of Columbia is to be absorbed into the states of Maryland and Virginia (Section 13).
22. The Federal government is required to pay the state or local governments remuneration for the services they provide to federal facilities (Section 13).
23. Federal lands are to be surrendered to the control of the states (Section 17).

Article 2: The Presidency
1. Candidates for the Presidency and Vice Presidency are required to prove natural-born citizen status (Section1).
2. Presidential nominations, if not acted on by Congress in three months, are to be considered approved (Section 2).
3. No treaty made with a foreign power is to usurp the provisions of this constitution (Section 2).
4. Presidential briefing on classified programs.

Article 3: Supreme Court
1. The number of justices making up the court is defined (Section 1).
2. A term limit of fifteen years is imposed for Court justices (Section 1).
3. The definition of treason is amended (Section 3).
4. The death penalty is recognized as a viable punishment (Section 4).
5. Crimes for which the death penalty can be given are defined (Section 4).
6. Accepted methods of execution are defined (Section 4).
7. Congressional ethics violations are to be investigated by a standing committee appointed by the Chief Justice of the Supreme Court and

reporting to the Supreme Court (Section 5).
Article 4: Relationships among the States, Admission of New States, and Responsibilities of the Federal Government to the States.

No major changes here.

Article 5: Procedures for Amending the Constitution.

Only minor changes here.

Article 6: Supreme Law of the Land.

No major changes here.

Article 7: Means for Ratification of the New Constitution

No major changes here.

EPILOGUE

I am sure that there will be detractors who will want to use a new constitution to fix what they feel are the wrongs of society. Many social issues, such as but not limited to abortion or gay rights, do not belong here. A constitution by definition is a _framework of government_ and not a bucket to throw into everything one feels is wrong with society. I tried to adhere to this principle. Those societal issues should be handled by statuary law and not the constitution.

We presently stand on a ledge looking back over two thousand years of human struggle for freedom and the right of self-determination, as well as the last two hundred years of our own history. Stretching below us is the path we have taken. Sometimes it was clear, and at other times, very rocky. From the failure of our forefathers to ban slavery, which resulted in a bloody civil war, to the failure to grant women equal rights and so on, issues have been resolved through blood, debate, and amendment. Turning around and viewing the scene ahead of us, we see that the path divides into two directions. One path leads onward and upward to a better future, and the other leads to a fog-shrouded valley. If we do nothing regarding the foundation of our society, the unfortunate consequence will be a walk into that fog-shrouded valley, and eventually we will become lost, scattered, and I predict the union will dissolve. The acid that dissolves us will be crushing debt. If, however, we choose to overhaul our foundation to make it stronger, then we shall continue moving upward to a bright future. This period will then be looked upon as just one of the rocky parts of our historical past.

INDEX

A

Amendment Eight: 27
Amendment Eighteen: 28
Amendment Eleven: 27
Amendment Fifteen: 28
Amendment Five: 26
Amendment Four: 25
Amendment Fourteen: 27
Amendment Nine: 27
Amendment Nineteen: 28
Amendment One: 24
Amendment Seven: 26
Amendment Seventeen: 28
Amendment Six: 26
Amendment Sixteen: 28
Amendment Ten: 27
Amendment Thirteen: 27
Amendment Thirty One: Proposed: Compulsory purchases 31
Amendment Thirty: Proposed: Corporate taxes 31
Amendment Three: 25
Amendment Twelve: 27
Amendment Twenty Eight: Proposed: Terrorist tribunals 30
Amendment Twenty Five: 29
Amendment Twenty Four: 29
Amendment Twenty Nine: Proposed: Peoples right to be protected from
    predators. 30
Amendment Twenty One: 29

Amendment Twenty Seven: Proposed: Entitlement programs 29
Amendment Twenty Six: 29
Amendment Twenty Three: 29
Amendment Twenty Two: 29
Amendment Twenty: 28
Amendment Two: 25
approval process 23
arms 25
Article 1 1
Article 2 16
Article 3 19
Article 4 21
Article 5 22
Article 6 22
Article 7 23

B

bail 27
bankruptcies 13
Bill of Attainder 15
BILL OF RIGHTS 24
budget 10

C

census 2
Classified Programs 18
coast guard 13
coin and print money 10
Congressional Term limits 2
currency of the United States 10

D

Death of the President or Vice President 6
death penalty 20
Deem & Pass 3
determination of state districts 2
District of Columbia 14
duration of the election campaign 5

E

ear marks 3
elections for the President, Vice President 5
entitlement programs 29
ethics codes 16
ethics violations 20

executive power 16

F

Federal lands 16
filibustering 3
flat rate individual income tax 9
framework of government 35

G

gerrymandering 2

H

House of Representatives 1
House of Representatives are to be elected at large .2

I

impeachment. 4
indictment of a Grand Jury 26
insolvent corporations 13
ITEMS IN THIS NEW CONSTITUTION 32

J

judge of the Elections 8
judicial power 19

L

legislative powers 1
licenses for the carrying of concealed firearms. 25

M

majority popular vote 16
Medicaid and Medicare 29
method of execution 20
military tribunal 30

N

natural born citizen 16
naturalization 12
News media 5
number of representatives 2

O

oath or affirmation 17

P

parochial schools 24
Polling places 5
post office 12
President of the House 3
prisoners of war 30
public debt 28
public trial 26

R

Regulation of Commerce 16
religion 24
repeated nor multiple appeals 26
Reprieves and Pardons 17
revenue 9
right of citizens of the United States to vote 16
right to appeal 26

S

searches and seizures 25
self protection 25
Self-Extracting-Rule 3
sexual predators 30
Social Security 29
state legislatures 2
stolen firearms 25
suits at common law 26

T

tax 9
term limit for the Supreme Court 19
terrorists 30
Title of Nobility 15
to big to fail 13
Treason 20
treaties, ...17

U

unfounded mandates 10

W

war 13
Warrants 25
waterways 13
weapons of an obvious military nature 25
Writ of Habeas Corpus 15

www.ingramcontent.com/pod-product-compliance
Lightning Source LLC
Chambersburg PA
CBHW060651290526
45793CB00001B/487